IMAGES
of England

PEACEHAVEN

SONG

COME TO PEACEHAVEN!

Words by **GEORGE ASAF** Music by **FELIX POWELL**

Author and Composer of

"PACK UP YOUR TROUBLES IN
YOUR OLD KIT BAG!"

With the Compliments of the
South Coast Land and Resort Co., Ltd.,
4, Vernon Place, London, W.C.1.,
Proprietors of the Peacehaven Estates.

One of the new settlers at the new Garden City was Felix Powell, best known perhaps for writing 'Pack up your troubles in your old kit bag'. He was befriended by Charles Neville who prevailed upon him to write a number of songs about Peacehaven. 'Come to Peacehaven!' is probably the best known of these. George Asaf was the pen name of George Powell, brother of Felix.

IMAGES
of England

PEACEHAVEN

Compiled by
Tony Payne

TEMPUS

First published 2000
Copyright © Tony Payne, 2000

Tempus Publishing Limited
The Mill, Brimscombe Port,
Stroud, Gloucestershire, GL5 2QG

ISBN 0 7524 1659 6

Typesetting and origination by
Tempus Publishing Limited
Printed in Great Britain by
Midway Clark Printing, Wiltshire

This volume is dedicated to those who go down to the sea in ships and occupy their business in great waters: the Lifeboatmen.

Contents

Introduction

I have spent over two thirds of my life in Peacehaven, having gone to that most individual of places to start work back in 1951. It would be quite unfair to say that my affection for Peacehaven is well known and that I have stood up for the place more times than I can remember. If I am perfectly honest there have been many times when I have to admit that Peacehaven perhaps needs apologizing for – but I always seemed to manage to disguise this with a well-intentioned love of the place.

When talking to Mr 'Joe Public' it seems as though everyone I speak to knows all about Peacehaven and its history: how it all started, how it stemmed from a series of competitions and promotions, how its founder was a Canadian 'shyster' who came here with a small fortune and how the town was built with funds filched from soldiers of the First World War who bought fraudulent bonds and so on. All wrong, of course, but nevertheless a lot of the stigma stuck.

It was because of this misinformation that I have, over the years, attempted to put the record straight. In 1987 I produced a mainly pictorial book which set out to tell how the village grew through the interwar years under the direction of its founder, Charles William Neville. It told of the hard times as well as the good times; it also told how countless difficulties were overcome and the attacks by what Neville called his 'traducers' and a 'little band of Bolsheviks'. I think that those old 'Arcadians' had much to be proud of and the new 'Arcadians' have much to envy from the early days. In my quest for facts I had the luck to be a good friend of Roderick Neville Jnr, the grandson of Charles Neville, and through Rod I learned much about the early days.

When it became obvious to all that Spain had every intention of invading England in the sixteenth century, Parliament gave instructions to Sir Thomas Palmer and Sir Walter Covert to prepare a map of the South Coast showing their recommendations for fortifying the shores with armaments, entrenchments and the like. We find that at what we now know as Peacehaven there was an early settlement named Moredale referred to as a 'stead', or more correctly a 'farmstead'. This settlement appears to have been located at what we today call Steyning Avenue at its junction with the Promenade. The appended footnotes give more detail but it is obvious from the report that it was thought that Moredale was worth fortifying.

Crossing from east to west there was, in later times, the Dover Road (now the A259 South Coast Road) and another road led north from today's Bolney Avenue to join the Lewes Road. There was a very sombre reminder of the times at the 'Gallows Hill' (just to the east of Hoddern Farm). In the nineteenth century the Hoddern Tollgate (or Paygate) was situated at the eastern end of today's Peacehaven and at the western end, at Portobello, there could be found the Coastguard Cottages, built in the early 1830s for the new Coastguard Service which came into being when the Coast Blockade for the Prevention of Smuggling ended.

At the nearby town and seaport of Newhaven there was based a sizeable man-o'-war, HMS *Hyperion*, with six attendant cutters. Opposite the site of the Coastguard houses was the then newly rebuilt and refurbished ex-Lifeboat Inn, the property of one William Balcombe Langridge, a notary public from Lewes. This was taken under the control of the Comptroller of Customs for use as a control centre. The original inn was built around 1765 and was rebuilt over a period of time around fifty years later. The owner, William Balcombe Langridge (who also owned lands in the district), was very concerned with the dreadful loss of life from shipwreck which occurred all along the coast. He was the keeper of the 'Protest Books' for the area. These wonderful volumes contained statements and depositions from those who had been shipwrecked or similarly endangered. It was because of this interest that Langridge later envisaged having a form of life-car stationed at the inn.

One of the earliest buildings in Peacehaven was the old Shepherd's Cot which is situated in today's Comptes. It is a listed building and was one of many such 'cots' that stretched across the downs in the great days of sheep farming. The South Downs were home to thousands of sheep and great sheep fairs were held at Findon Lewes and other centres. These cots gave shelter to shepherds and sick or injured sheep during rough weather and they were erected every fifteen miles or so across the downs. The next cot from here is at Birling Gap.

The founder of Peacehaven and indeed Saltdean was Charles William Neville. He was born in 1881 in Darlington to parents who made their living from exhibition work, including the 1898 Paris Exhibition. They were both fluent linguists, widely travelled and certainly aware of the benefits to be drawn from good publicity and advertising. It is easy to see where Charles got his flair and talent, which he soon put to good use.

At the outbreak of the First World War work stopped on the estates, by now stretching from Rottingdean to Friars Bay and onwards to Newhaven Valley and Riverside, but Neville and his staff went on about their business of marketing the estate. Charles Neville instituted a detailed scheme for marketing the area to get round his lack of capital. He founded the South Coast Land & Resort Company, with offices in Vernon Place, London. He took as a fellow director of the company Charles Gold who was to be the Company Architect and the driving force behind the development of new estates after the war. Charles Neville had a dislike of solicitors and so with one swift stroke he changed the system of land transfer by preparing a pro forma conveyance. All you had to do was fill in the blank spaces with names and details of plot and block numbers and draw a site plan of the land to be conveyed. This did not go down well with the legal profession!

Meanwhile Charles William Neville continued to buy land in the ever-growing area of 'Greater Peacehaven' as he called his empire, which now stretched from Newhaven through the River estate, the Valley estate, Newhaven Heights estate, Blakeney Heights estate, Harbour Heights, Peacehaven itself, the Annexe estates, Telscombe Cliffs, the Beach estate (what we now call Bannings Vale), Saltdean Estate, Rottingdean Heights and Parts of Rottingdean itself. The estates even reached the banks of the River Ouse, which became the site of the Peacehaven Riverside Wharf.

Neville always spoke, even in the earliest days, of the forthcoming Peacehaven Light Railway Company which would have been a boon to many. In the *Peacehaven Post* (a house magazine) of August 1922 mention is made of negotiations, the result of which would be published shortly. It is a fact that an area of land was set aside and delineated on early plans as 'railway reservations'. It is a little-known fact that in the 1866 Parliamentary Sessions an enabling act was sought to provide a railway from Brighton to Ovingdean, Rottingdean, Telscombe, Piddinghoe, Newhaven and Denton. A similar act was applied for an extension to Seaford and thence to Eastbourne. Nothing came of these, but detailed plans still exist.

The early 'Arcadians' came to Peacehaven for a number of diverse reasons; most would agree that they liked the absence of interference from local government. Neville's view was that this lack of interference was of utmost importance and therefore sought to 'do his own thing' when he was frustrated by lack of co-operation from the authorities. You could in those 'salad days' buy your little corner of England very cheaply and you could build what you liked where you liked (within reason). As well as paying over a period of time, you could build over a period of time. The Estate Company would do all it could to help you build your own home. The Estate Company had a very large builders' yard together with workshops and they encouraged those interested in DIY to come along on a Sunday to use the Company's woodworking and other machines, all for nothing. These early settlers were prepared to accept the lack of metalled roads in the same way that they were prepared to accept quite primitive drainage and the lack of street lighting. It was not until later when a group of strong-minded people got together and made their voices heard. They demanded 'improvements' immediately. There was so much feeling being generated at this time that Neville said that there were times when he feared for his safety when visiting the estate.

From the outset the Estate Company did all that it could to provide a variety of new properties of varying designs. Many plan books were produced with hundreds of designs to choose from, all at low prices. The aim was, of course, to prevent outside builders coming onto the estate and taking a slice of the rich pickings to be gained. Those who tried would more often than not find themselves in court on the grounds of non-compliance with the company conditions of purchase. Eventually outside builders did arrive and they got their fair share of the work going on then. Some of the plans of the new homes for the returning heroes are amazing in their design. The 'Exeter' was supposedly a compact and comfortable home – compact is an understatement! The whole building measured just 20ft by 18ft, the size of a reasonable lounge today. In this space was squeezed a 9ft 3in by 12ft living room, a 9ft 3ins by 7ft bedroom, a 9ft 3in kitchen and that was all – no bath, no WC. The cost was £360. At the top end of the scale was the 'Denby', which boasted a living room, a dining room, a large kitchen, two bedrooms and a porch but still no bathroom.

Charles William Neville died at his home at his home in Rottingdean in 1959. His description of Peacehaven as a 'Garden City by the sea' was not intended merely as a picturesque name. 'Garden City' was the term used at the time of Peacehaven's inception for what is known today as a 'new town'. It was a system, not a place. Welwyn Garden City is one of the best known of these developments. In a Garden City everything was owned by a freeholder who then let the various parts.

From these very humble yet turbulent beginnings Peacehaven has grown and prospered to become something like the Garden City by the Sea that Neville dreamed of, in spite of all. You could list Peacehaven's faults for as long as you like but people still want to settle here – and who can blame them? It is quite probable that if Neville were demonstrating his enterprise today, he would receive far more recognition for his work.

Acknowledgements

Most importantly I have to thank all of the people who have given so generously of their time, their effort and their prized photographs etc.

I would particularly like to thank Jim Palmer, an old Peacehaven Pioneer and good friend, Dorothy Penn and Jack Wagstaff for their reminiscences of the early days. Where I have been unable to name individuals on the illustrations I apologize in advance. Most of the photographs come from my own collection but I have to give a 'blanket' thank-you to all the others who have helped. Lastly, but certainly not least, thanks to Jacky Burton for coping with my terrible handwriting and making sense with the typescript.

Tony Payne

One

Charles Neville and His Vision

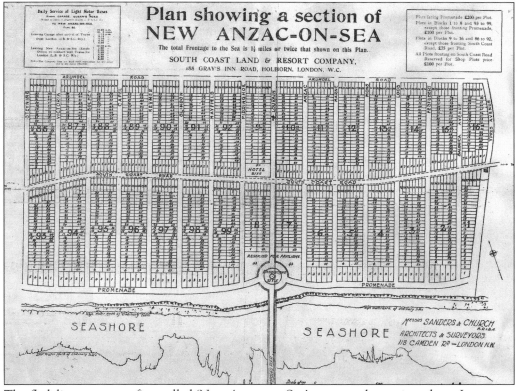

Plan showing a section of
NEW ANZAC-ON-SEA
The total Frontage to the Sea is 1½ miles or twice that shown on this Plan.

SOUTH COAST LAND & RESORT COMPANY,
188 GRAY'S INN ROAD, HOLBORN, LONDON, W.C.

Plots facing Promenade £200 per Plot.
Plots in Blocks 1 to 8 and 93 to 99,
except those fronting Promenade,
£100 per Plot.
Plots in Blocks 9 to 16 and 86 to 92,
except those fronting South Coast
Road, £75 per Plot.
All Plots fronting on South Coast Road
Reserved for Shop Plots price
£100 per Plot.

SEASHORE

SEASHORE

Messrs SANDERS & CHURCH
ARCHITECTS & SURVEYORS,
118 CAMDEN R⁰ —LONDON N.W.

The fledgling town was first called 'New Anzac-on-Sea', a name chosen in a draw. It was not long before this name proved not to be universally popular and it was soon changed to Peacehaven. This is a very early plan of the town when still known as New Anzac and it shows just a section of the estate. There are sites for a pier, pavilions and bandstands. Many of the roads at the eastern end of the estate are named after First World War battles. These names, too, were later changed to the names used today. What has remained unchanged is the basic grid system, clearly seen on the plan, which allowed the maximum number of plots to fit onto the minimum area of land.

Charles William Neville was born in Darlington in 1881 to parents who were astute business people who made their money from the promotion of exhibitions. They were widely travelled and accomplished linguists. Charles was also widely travelled, having worked in Canada and Australia, mainly in property and land. In those countries, as in England, his efforts often attracted attention from the press, not all of it favourable. He came to Peacehaven just before the start of the First World War and he purchased land from various landowners (initially some 415 acres at £15 per acre).

Charles' lands at Peacehaven eventually extended to 700 acres. They included the three Hoddern farms (seen on this early map), which were incorporated into the layout of Peacehaven. The first task was to map out and then set out the estate with individual plots measuring 25ft by 100ft. The often criticized estate layout used a grid system with roads running east to west and avenues north to south. No attempt was made to set out the town with sympathy for the changing contours of the land. The grid system meant simply that the maximum number of plots could be included and maximum return on the investment made.

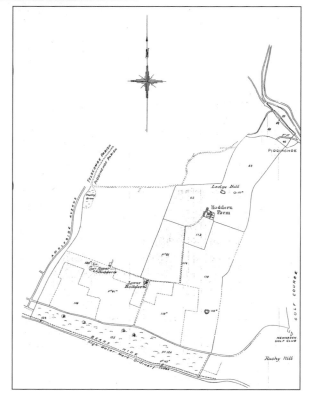

When Charles Neville purchased the lands that were to become Peacehaven he took over an aerial landing ground with associated buildings. These buildings were to be invaluable to the new estate. The landing ground was part of a chain of seaplane and aeroplane stations set up by the Admiralty to combat German submarines in the Channel. This station covered some 50 acres in all and stretched from Ambleside Avenue to Roderick Avenue and from Arundel Road to Firle Road. There were two large sheds for aircraft storage and other smaller buildings on the site. The aircraft used were six De Havilland DH6s like the one seen here. Earlier still there had been a 'Kite' section on the site and it was also used for balloons. It was Neville's plan to promote air travel and recreation from this site; in the 1930s pleasure flights were given and the landing ground was advertised as a great amenity.

To continue the aerial input, when the luxurious Hotel Peacehaven was opened Neville engaged the services of Anton Fokker, the famous Dutch aviator, to demonstrate his new 'glider', the first time that such an event had been seen by the public in England. The wind was not right for successful gliding at Peacehaven and the demonstration took place at Saltdean, then part of 'Greater Peacehaven'. The *Daily Mail* had engaged Fokker's services for later in the same month and they never forgave Charles Neville for 'upstaging' them. The hangars eventually became the Company block-making works and the dreams of a Peacehaven aerodrome went unfulfilled.

The Peacehaven River Estate had a substantial and commercially very attractive river frontage at Newhaven. This became the Peacehaven Riverside Wharf and people were encouraged to believe that the new town actually had a harbour. The Company acquired a small sailing ship, the *Lord Hartington*, which was busily engaged in bringing to England bricks, titles and other building materials at a time when they were in short supply in England. The Wharf was on what is today's Robinson Road; it served Peacehaven well for a long time.

The International Friendship Camp in the valley at north Peacehaven. This body was established by Mr Noel Ede (brother of the Labour politician) and still exists today. It advocates working and playing together to foster understanding. The valley was originally set aside for smallholdings. The Company actually encouraged fur and feather farming, stating that it was the new way to make money. To help keep the 'settlers' happy, the Company gave free use of a lorry to take produce to and from Brighton market. This part of Peacehaven was very much the 'Arcadia' sought by so many after the First World War. There is still an air of 'rurality' in today's valley.

Oxen were used for ploughing on the burgeoning estate alongside horses and mechanical means. Mr George Rodhouse, a valued Company servant, told of how he had to remove three standing stones from the farm trackway above Micheldene pit. It took two whole teams of oxen to drag them out of the ground. The Peacehaven and Telscombe Historical Society hopes to locate these standing stones and re-erect them at some appropriate spot.

The Cliffs, Peacehaven.

Telscombe Cliffs, with the old Coastguard Cottages, Comptroller of Customs' house and sewage works beyond. In the early days much was made of the wonderful sea and cliff-top views. However, the bleakness and desolation of much of Peacehaven, coupled with the lack of amenities, brought a lot of trouble for the new company when a number of plot owners brought a case against Neville and his company. They claimed that they had been misled by advertising and empty promises. In court, the judge found for the plot owners and ordered Neville to refund their money. The judgement was overturned at a later hearing.

ALONG THE CLIFFS. PEACEHAVEN.

A similar location as the previous photograph but a few years later. Numerous new houses have been built, steps have been constructed to the beach and public shelters have been erected on the 'prom'. The scene has changed considerably since this photograph too; sea and wind erosion has removed much of the cliff-top promenade and coastal defence works have halted the slide only in the last few years.

The steps to the beach and the 'bastion' provided a much-wanted leisure amenity. A salt-water pool flushed by the tide was soon incorporated and proved a great asset in the early days; this pool fell into disrepair during the war and was never rebuilt. Space was provided for a new pool when the coastal defences were built, but as yet nothing has come of it. A relic of the past was uncovered during a particularly strong storm in the late 1960s when a fall of chalk revealed an old well which ran right down to the beach – this could date from the old settlement of Moredale.

Before the construction of the coastal defences the cliffs receded greatly, but the problem is now reduced. At the bottom of the steps is the bastion and the early pool, which was well used, despite the lack of covering and heating. The cliffs at Peacehaven suffer the ravages of the 'longshore drift', which is best described as the cutting of the base of the cliff by the waves which break on the beach at an angle. This works away at the base of the cliff and eventually causes many tons of chalk to fall. This action can be seen on a rough day when, with a high tide, the waves run along the cliff for considerable distances.

The earliest steps were primitive indeed, with not even a handrail for support or safety. This did not stop many hundreds of people coming down to the beach for a swim, for relaxation, or just to pass the time of day. After a storm, the pickings from the beach can be rich in all respects but the biggest problem is carrying driftwood and the like up the many steps to the top. On the beach there are pools containing plentiful supplies of prawns and winkles – this rich harvest was not neglected by the settlers.

The strong south-westerly winds then, as now, took their toll and many people moved back from the cliff top because of this. This lorry is loaded with saplings to be planted as a windbreak, but this idea of Neville's was only partially successful as many of the newly planted trees were uprooted or killed by the wind.

The first building to be erected was a large asbestos hut used as an estate office and builders' store. Neville said that he spent many lonely nights here in the formative days but at least it provided shelter. As the estate grew, offices also grew and appeared all over the place. The original building became the Rosemary Tea Rooms and Dairy, a focal point in early Peacehaven. It was later taken over by the Thorntons and became the first Village Hall and meeting place. It was here in 1922 that the young Miss Flora Robson gave her first two public dramatic recitations. The building saw many more changes and eventually went on to become a nursery. It was pulled down during the Peacehaven revival to make way for a terrace of five houses. There is a plaque on the wall of the westernmost house to remind us of the Rosemary and Miss Flora Robson.

The A259 South Coast Road, looking west. On the right is Tudor House, a tea rooms and general store. In the 1980s it was even said to be the base for 'ladies of doubtful virtue'! The main road is still unmetalled and also very narrow. The flat-roofed building on the left is now called Meridian Lodge but was previously known as Gladden's Corner House. Mr Gladden was an early Peacehaven builder. A third storey and a pitched roof were added some years later.

One of the earliest pioneer Arcadians was Mr Isaac Henry Wagstaff. He came to Peacehaven in 1911, before Mr Neville had arrived on the scene. He settled in what later became known as Cissbury Avenue; at that time there were a number of smallholdings established but earning a living from the land was not easy, so Mr Wagstaff worked at the Newhaven Marine Workshops. It was not until the estate had started to grow and burgeon that he purchased the building shown here. The building's previous use as an army hut is very apparent. The business has since grown to become one of the town's foremost business enterprises.

Most of the surrounding countryside was bare and barren. Sheepfold Farm was a small farming unit adjoining what was then the moribund early Newhaven Golf Course. Mr Neville purchased the golf course and the early clubhouse (which used to be on the coast side of the road) as part of the new town's attractions. There were originally nine holes on each side of the main road but Neville retained only the nine holes on the north side of the road, built a new clubhouse and kept the remainder of the land for future building. The gorse grew in profusion everywhere.

Mr and Mrs Sangster were valued Company agents and were well liked in the town. They ran one of the numerous estate agencies in the town, which were positioned so as to maximize business and reduce competition from outside firms.

One of the earliest amenities that the Company provided was the Pavilion cinema. This stood on the south side of the coast road in the north-eastern corner of today's 'Dell'. It was well patronized and showed all the latest 'talkies'. It was also used as a live theatre and many extravagant musical shows were performed here mainly by the Peacehaven Philharmonic, which achieved a good deal of success in the area. For many years it was run and managed by Mr David Fowler, a popular early Peacehavener who supported the town in many ways. The premises burned down in 1940 and were never rebuilt.

A 'montage' postcard portrays well the beach and cliff-top attractions of Peacehaven. The pool was lost during the Second World War and, like so many other amenities, it was never rebuilt.

The old Dover Road, later to become the A259, was originally part of a greater turnpike road. Tollgates such as this (at the eastern end of Peacehaven, near Cornwall Avenue) were set up at intervals to collect travellers' dues. A reader of the *Peacehaven Post* remembers being brought up here in a family of ten. The lady of the house kept the gate for 3s 6d per week. In earlier days the tollgate well was the only source of fresh drinking water, which was available for 6d per bucket. It was also much frequented by the local smuggling fraternity who used it as a meeting place. A document recording 'Auction Sale particulars' advises that in 1829 a Debenture for £1,000 was secured on these tolls. The next tollgate was at Ovingdean crossroads.

Gordon Volk, son of Magnus Volk of Volk's Railway fame, was the artist employed by the Company to portray all that was best in the Garden City. He was, without a doubt, a very fine artist, although not averse to a little bit of artistic licence. This view from the back of Peacehaven towards Seaford shows all that was good about the town: lots of land, superb sea and downland views, clear skies and lovely countryside. It worked – of course.

Two
Promotions, Competitions and Gordon Volk

Neville also developed Saltdean, where he ensured that the mistakes made at Peacehaven were not repeated. Drains were put in where Peacehaven had to make do with cesspools, roads were properly surfaced and streets were laid out following the contours of the land instead of the unfriendly 'grid' system. This building was advertised widely as being the 'Free Gift House' for 1925, valued at £1,125. The public were told that the house had been won by a grateful Miss Jackson from West Norwood. It is unclear why in the 1950s the 'free' house was opened as an estate office by a subsidiary of the Saltdean Estate Company which took over the assets of the old South Coast Land and Resort Co. and the Peacehaven Estates.

**THIS SEASIDE HOME, COMPLETELY FURNISHED,
VALUE £1,200
WILL BE GIVEN AWAY DURING 1927**

This is the 1927 Gift House. The property was one of two built to form a 'gateway' to the new Harbour Heights and Peacehaven Heights estates. Gordon Volk, the Company artist, has done himself proud; the actual property can still be seen today but has been somewhat extended. The background views are not quite what is shown but the bungalow is readily identifiable.

Every edition of the Company's house magazine, *Peacehaven Post* (later the *Downland Post*), was liberally dotted with promotional drawings by Gordon Volk. This is one of the first properties on the Beach Estate, sited at what is known today as Bannings Vale. The price of £350 would have been attractive to many, considering the fine locality. In the background is the coast road and the easily identifiable cliff-top opposite the old Kittiwake Hotel; the views from the lower end of the estate are first class.

The Gift House for 1926 was sited in Ambleside Avenue. The cliff-top and sea are actually further away than this impression suggests. Charles Neville's intention was to make the entire country aware of his Peacehaven estates by the annual Gift House award. They were doubtless a lure to many seeking retirement homes or just somewhere to live away from the hustle and bustle of city life. All who purchased land on the estates had their names entered into the annual draw which was conducted with great publicity and celebrations.

This is said to be the actual 1926 Gift House. It is not quite as advertised and illustrated above, but is nevertheless a first-class home for retirement.

THE CROFT,
EDENBRIDGE.
KENT.

To the Secretary   11-8-27
Peacehaven Estates Ltd
Dear Sir
        I am glad to state how pleased I am with
the Presentation Gift House which I was lucky enough
to win in your recent competition —
It is an ideal one for seaside residence, is very
substantially built + excellently furnished by Maples
Maples of London —
        I am sure the view over the Sea + Downs could not
be excelled anywhere along the South Coast, whilst
frequent 'bus service to both Newhaven + Brighton
makes it possible to get to London within a
very short time —

As a bracing, healthy, residential place,
Peacehaven in my opinion can not be excelled
+ I have every reason to think, that within a
few years the whole of the coast between
Newhaven + Brighton will be the great
goal of health seeking Londoners + others —
                        Yours faithfully
                        C.W.H. Brewington.

This letter is supposedly from the happy and lucky winner of the Presentation Gift House. It may be the case that this was written with publicity in mind and not just by a contended 'punter' – it is very carefully worded. Either way, it was a fine way to gain publicity and support.

Gordon Volk at his best! His task was to show to the country the main road of the new Garden City, but the spacious, wide, tree-lined South Coast Road shown here may seem at variance with the photographs of the road elsewhere in this volume. The four pylons marking the gateway to the Garden City estate were built and three still exist today; the other was 'helped' to fall down when the garage was built at the western end of the estate. There are far more people on the pavements and road than would be imaginable today.

These 'Live by the Sea' posters appeared on every railway station in the country during the formative years of the Garden City and 'Uncle Reub' was almost a household friend. If you were trying to escape the travails of everyday life, the privations of the recent war and being dependent on somebody else, then what better thing to do than get a southbound train to Peacehaven? You were offered rest and recreation, a chance to have your own home for a deposit of just £50 – and no wicked landlords looking over your shoulder.

Gordon Volk came into his own when portraying the future instead of the present. This is something the camera, no matter how carefully used, cannot portray. The Light Railway was talked about all the time and the *Peacehaven Post* often told of 'plans now being well advanced for the forthcoming link with the main railway system'. Land was set aside at North Peacehaven and shown on the estate plans as the 'railway reservation'. Mr Kearney, an Australian gentleman who settled at the Garden City, had been involved in railways in Australia and was working tirelessly on his 'Kearney Electric Light Railway'. He averred that he saw no reason why, when his railway was complete, residents could not get from the Garden City to London in 35 minutes!

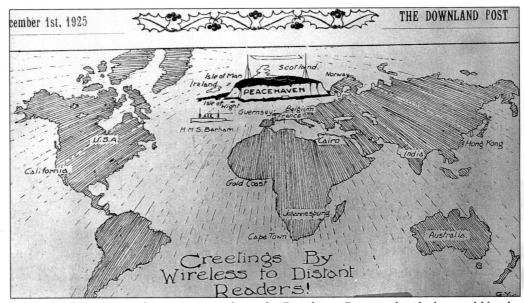

When the domestic wireless was in its infancy the *Peacehaven Post* wondered who would be the first to have a wireless installed at Peacehaven. When Mark Blakeney Pizzey acquired a 'complete installation' at his cliff-top home on the Promenade it became a talking point. This drawing infers that Peacehaven might be the home of radio broadcasting by sending 'greetings by wireless' to the world.

The burgeoning town by now took in all the various 'Heights' estates and this view overlooking Newhaven harbour shows the sites of Gibbon Road, Southdown Road, Northdown Road. There is the usual profusion of gorse on the top of the hill.

Until 1923 Peacehaven did not have its own council but was administered by Newhaven Urban and then Chailey Rural Councils. Gordon Volk shows us the team that he looked for in the forthcoming elections, detailing the members' outlook and policies. As the town grew over the years so did the council in its stature and there is little doubt that today's council has much to be proud about.

From the very beginning Peacehaven had a natural attribute on its very doorstep: the sea and the associated beaches. True, the beaches were mainly rock, as they are today, but the big drawback was that there was no access. There was a natural fissure through the cliffs at the bottom of today's Steyning Avenue. This was the site of the earlier Moredale settlement. This is Volk's impression of the steps before they were built; the pavilions at the top never materialized.

27

This is a page from one of the earliest brochures for the estate. The allegorical figure at the top is 'Brighton's fairest sister', as Peacehaven was named. The centre illustration shows a beach but no cliffs, as well as the ubiquitous trees so desired by Charles Neville. We see aeroplanes in the sky which was a reference to Neville's wish to see aerial pursuits as part of Peacehaven everyday life. Above all, it offers the call of 'health and happiness for all'.

FREE GIFT OF A £1,125 HOUSE AND SITE ON WHICH IT STANDS !!

PEACEHAVEN

THE SOUTH COAST RESORT ALMOST FIVE MILES IN LENGTH FACING THE SEA.

To mark another anniversary of the birth of Peacehaven the promoters are making two great offers to those who purchase Freehold Land there between April 9th and October 31st, 1925. (1) Free Gift of a £1,125 Freehold House and Site on which it stands. (2) £5 Free Offer to Every Reader.

FROM a Garden City by the Sea Peacehaven is rapidly becoming a Seaside Resort of the first magnitude. It is almost five miles in length, facing the sea, and is acknowledged to be the greatest Seaside town planning and land development enterprise yet undertaken in this country. In a little over four years Peacehaven has grown from a hamlet of 24 residents to a busy, thriving sea coast resort, comprising approximately 8,500 people. There is no doubt that the ideal situation of Peacehaven, in the heart of Downland, within a short bus ride from Brighton, and just over an hour's journey from London, together with its wonderful, invigorating, health-promoting air, and rich, fertile soil, have contributed to its unique success.

HOW TO SECURE OUR £1,125 FREEHOLD HOUSE and Site on which it stands, FREE.

This Offer is open to all. The Presentation House can be seen by visitors to Peacehaven at any time, and is ideally situated on Plots 17 and 18 in Chichester Drive, Saltdean, one of the choicest sections of the Peacehaven Estates.

It is a two-storey building, containing a large living room with bay windows, three bedrooms, bathroom, lavatory, kitchen, larder, and other domestic accommodations. It is a real labour-saving home, water laid on, ready for immediate occupation, and is immensely admired by all who have seen it. The tiled pavement and beautiful garden are in course of preparation and will be a source of inspiration.

Magnificent views of Downland and the English Channel can be obtained from its windows, and the famous Saltdean sandy beach is near by. Within 200 yards there is a frequent service of buses passing on the Brighton Road. By bus Brighton is only a 20 minutes' journey, while Rottingdean can be reached in five minutes, and Newhaven Town in 15 minutes.

THE SIMPLE CONDITIONS

THE ATTRACTIONS OF PEACEHAVEN.

A permanent way at a cost of several thousands of pounds has been made from the cliff to the foreshore, so that children and others can easily and quickly get to the sea for bathing and the joys of rock-pools and beach. In its corporate and civic life Peacehaven possesses an abounding vitality. It has many shops and tea gardens, and Hotel Peacehaven, for its size, is the most beautiful, convenient and up-to-date on the South Coast. Peacehaven has four churches, a College and school, a splendid dance hall, and a theatre and cinema. There are tennis courts, an excellent golf course, bowling greens, and a cricket field, an open space of almost 200 acres, a park of 18 acres, and several smaller recreation grounds. There are a flourishing Literary and Debating Society, a Philharmonic and Dramatic Society, Tennis Clubs, Bowling Clubs, &c., &c. There is a local newspaper, "The Peacehaven Gazette," and a monthly magazine, "The Downland Post and Sussex Magazine."

HOW TO GET THERE.

You can get to Peacehaven by train from London Bridge or Victoria to Brighton or Newhaven Town Station, and there is a frequent bus service from the Aquarium, Brighton, or from Newhaven. Our motor conveyance meets at Brighton Station the trains leaving Victoria daily at 11.5 a.m. and 12.5 p.m. Our visitors are taken direct to Peacehaven without charge, where our representatives will welcome you and place every facility at your disposal to assist you with your investigations.

WHAT YOU MUST DO TO-DAY.

Fill in this coupon to-day and make a profitable investment. There is a limit to the Freehold building sites we have available at Peacehaven; and they are being taken up quickly. Take advantage of our two-fold Gift

Almost every issue of the early *Peacehaven Post* magazines held similar advertisements to this. Alongside the annual Gift House competition, there is an extra incentive to readers in the form of a £5 voucher to anyone investing in the estate.

The TWELVE "POSTS" of PEACEHAVEN

Another Gordon Volk special was the 'Twelve Posts of Peacehaven' which appeared in many advertisements, newspapers and magazines as well as the Company's own brochures. It speaks for itself but what is interesting is the licence that Volk continues to use to the Company's advantage.

Charles Neville engaged the services of Anton Fokker, the famous Dutch aviator, to mark the opening of the Hotel Peacehaven was opened in 1922. He also provided a special 'Peacehaven Express' train for the occasion. Neville forestalled the *Daily Mail* which had booked Fokker's services for a date later in the month. The *Daily Mail* staff never forgave Neville for upstaging them and a great deal of bad feeling was created. Fokker entertained the numerous guests with various demonstrations during the morning after which they were all invited to lunch at the new Hotel.

Advertisements such as this appeared in all the major newspapers of the day as well as being exhibited on buses, trains and railway stations. They extolled the virtues of home ownership – a bargain for just £50 deposit and the balance payable at £1 per week. The enquirer also could enter the great Free Gift Offer of a £1,125 house and the land upon which it stood.

The official opening of the first promenade shelter provided an excuse for a social gathering. If the Promenade itself was an attraction and an amenity, the shelters proved a boon to many. They were solidly built of wood on a solid concrete base by the Peacehaven Building & Supply Company. The main units were made in the Company workshops and erected on site. They had seats on all four sides with protection from the wind and rain. The old shelters had to be removed because of the erosion of the land on which they stood; some were replaced by less charming modern structures.

Three
Time for Tea

Tea at Peacehaven.

In early Peacehaven there is little doubt that the tea house had a more important place than the beer house. It took a long spell of development before the first off-licence was granted at the Pioneer Stores, and even longer for the first public house to appear. There were many tea houses and tea shops, always with the ubiquitous home made cakes. The 'Rosemary' tea gardens was much advertised and much patronized. The company artist made much of the *Peacehaven Post* to advertise the benefits of a spell in the sun, quiet contemplation and, hopefully, the consummation of all in the purchase of a bungalow. This is one of Volk's early drawings and has been much used since.

This easily identifiable property was originally built just as Offa House, containing a tea room, restaurant, guest house and roof garden. The garden did not succeed, no doubt because of the perverse Peacehaven winds, but the tea room prospered, as did the restaurant. The building was divided and later sold off as three separate units, Offa House, La France and The Castle restaurant. In the 1960s a full licence was granted and the property became just The Castle. It has been known under several names since, including Pickwick's Place, The Retreat and latterly The White Schooner. Long may it flourish.

The Beach Café was a popular tea room and cafeteria situated at the southern end of Steyning Avenue, next to the beach. It served Peacehaven well for a long time. In later years like so many others it expanded and was renamed the Green Parrot but this did not enjoy the same success as the Beach Café and it was sold into the private sector and is now a fine seaside home. The illustration shows the original Beach Café nearing completion.

Saltdean: urban sprawl has not yet reached the town in this view from the late 1920s. The old Coastguard houses can be seen, as can the Estate Office, soon to become the free Gift House before reverting to a Company office some decades later. Where today's lido tempts the holidaymaker with its blue water there was then a tennis court; where today's subway comes out to meet the beach approach was a row of pillars with ornamental cappings on the top. On the cliff-top south of the coast road is a new tea house, the Smugglers' Haunt, which opened for business in 1925. Much like the Peacehaven Rosemary it doubled as a meeting place, town hall etc. A big attraction was the veranda. The passing of the Smugglers' Haunt was sadly lamented.

'Poltesco' used to advertise itself as Peacehaven's first guest house. Teas were available daily with fresh cakes and pastries made on the premises. Its fine position on the South Coast Road opposite Offa House was very convenient. Today it is a fine bungalow that is easily recognized. This early photograph displays well the wattle fence (made on the site in the company yard).

One of the many assets of the Rosemary was the extensive gardens, shown here. Contemporary signs on the walls tell of the many functions held here. It can truly be said that this building was a cradle of Peacehaven's social life.

The interior of the Rosemary was spacious, well laid out, clean and very presentable. A place to sit in comfort and consider one's future in the Garden City.

This and the next three photographs show the Peacehaven Hotel. It was Charles Neville's idea to have a first-class hotel from the beginning. The property occupied one of the finest sites in the town, at Phyllis Avenue South. It enjoyed superb sea and cliff-top views and was built to a high standard. The cost then, in early 1920s, was alarmingly high: over £10,000 in total for the building work, with an additional £6,500 being lavished on the interior and furnishings. Neville agreed that perhaps 'Peacehaven was not yet ready fur such sumptuous premises'. This is the original first section of the hotel with the ornate rockeries just being laid out.

A small fortune was spent on the sunken 'Italianate' garden with superb rockeries, statuary, fountains, flowering shrubs, many seats for the weary passer-by, accommodation for band concerts and – of course – a 'tea pavilion'. It is interesting to note that this card was sold by Percy & Co., who occupied 'Percian House', now a small block of flats on the corner of Cairo Avenue North. The ubiquitous Company flag flies proudly above all. The property in the immediate background is called Karmit. The right half was originally the Company central estate office and the left half was opened by the first bank in the Garden City, Barclays. Further building works will be observed at the top right.

PEACEHAVEN HOTEL GARDENS.

The company built this huge greenhouse, heated of course, to grow salad stuffs and strawberries (it was said that 5,000 were planted in one day). The gardens are taking shape and wattle hurdles have been put up to provide shelter for plants and people alike. The hard surfaced area to the left of the building was known as 'the stand' and it was used by taxis, hire cars and the Peacehaven charabancs. One of the new Promenade shelters can be seen as well as the fenced off tennis courts to the south of the bowling greens. The Peacehaven Hotel was often referred to as 'the bungalow hotel for the bungalow city'.

Here the finished hotel and gardens stand in all their glory. The hotel was successful for many years and it later passed into private hands. One of the last owners was Mr Roger Lythgoe, a first-class restaurateur and a sound businessman. When he sold the property and business to the brewery the hotel was allowed to fall into disrepair and became a shadow of its former self. Squatters moved in and eventually the building was demolished and what can only be called a 'Glitz' palace was put up in its place. The garden was filled in to make way for a new development.

Four
Churches and
Monuments

Old maps show just to the north of Telscombe Tye on the old track to Pickershill Farm a monument known as Harvey's Stone or Harvey's Cross. John Harvey was an Army officer serving with the 9th Hussars. While on holiday in Sussex in 1802 he was out riding and died after being thrown from his horse. At first a plain stone was erected to mark the spot where he was thrown and later a more suitable stone cross on a stone and brick base was erected. The cross was damaged by military exercises during the Second World War and was all but forgotten. A local writer and resident of Saltdean, Mr Douglas D'Enno, spent some time investigating the story and he located the remains of the monument; it is now to be restored and re-erected thanks to his efforts.

At each end of the Peacehaven Estate Charles Neville planned to erect two monoliths, one each side of the road, to mark the gateways to the Garden City. These monoliths were erected around 1916 and originally they had signs reading 'New Anzac-on-Sea' (later changed to Peacehaven). When the monoliths were restored in the 1960s the signs were removed. The eastern 'Pylons' were just east of Cornwall Avenue and the western ones just west of Lincoln Avenue. Artex of Newhaven had the monoliths restored and repainted for the Queen's Jubilee in 1977. Close inspection of early photographs indicate that the eastern structures each had a gas lamp fixed to the top but these did not last long. One of the western pylons was demolished by a lorry during the construction of a garage.

An early Peacehaven resident, Cdr Davenport RN, realized that the new Garden City, lay on the line of the Greenwich Meridian and after discussion with Charles Neville, it was decided to make the most of this little bit of Peacehaven fame. A fine monument to mark the spot was proposed and funds were raised from the public to pay for the costs. The precursor to the monument stood on the Promenade astride a concrete strip that ran to the cliff edge. It showed distances to well-known capital cities on finger boards.

The finished monument was erected at a cost of £300. Much of this was raised by public subscription with £100 being donated anonymously. The event was marked with the usual celebrations and local luminaries were invited to attend the official opening which was introduced by the Astronomer Royal. Neville unveiled the monument on 10 August 1935. When the coastal defence works were carried out in the 1960s the monument was taken down stone by stone and re-erected some 30ft further north to allow work to take place on the cliff face.

The BMA Hazlecar was made at the Hazledean Garage which was at the junction of the South Coast Road with Telscombe Cliffs Way. It was an electric car powered with batteries made by the Battery Makers' Association from Brighton. It had a range of some 60 miles and the cost of £535 in 1952 coupled with a maximum speed of around 20mph meant that it was destined to fail. Only six were made and a seventh was fitted with a Ford 8 petrol motor but did not go into production. It was, perhaps, a glorious attempt that failed – but at least it was local.

One of the very earliest brick structures in the area was this little Shepherd's Cot, situated in today's Comptes. It measures 9ft by 6ft and is 6ft high; it originally had a dirt floor and a brick fireplace. These cots littered the South Downs and are a reminder of the times when sheep farming was widespread in Sussex. Cots fifteen or so miles apart gave a shepherd somewhere to take sick sheep and to find shelter for himself. The window is a much later addition. The building is now listed.

THE GRACIE FIELDS HOME AND ORPHANAGE. PEACEHAVEN.

Gracie Fields was an early resident of Peacehaven and she purchased a property in Dorothy Avenue for her father. This was later to become better known as the Gracie Fields Home and Orphanage. It catered also for children whose parents were absent for long periods. Today the property has been extended and is a Church home for the elderly and plays an important part in Peacehaven life.

Even before the Hotel Peacehaven was completed Mr Neville had commissioned Professor Vecchi of Florence to sculpt for him this marble statue of 'Peace' and it stood in the foyer of the hotel for many years. The statuary of the hotel is mentioned in Grahame Greene's novel *Brighton Rock*.

One of the earliest churches to be erected in Peacehaven was the Free Church, seen here in Mayfield Avenue. The Wagstaff family were prominent among the people involved in having the building erected and it performed trojan service before a new building was constructed on the South Coast Road and this building became a Church Hall. It still stands today and is widely used. The road shown here is fairly typical of the street quality in early Peacehaven.

The new Evangelical Free Church erected with the support of Peacehaveners such as the Wagstaff family. It served the needs of the growing Peacehaven for many years and it supported senior members and young alike. The author remembers 'Father Emeritus' Merritt, a pillar of the church in all respects.

New Church for Peacehaven
Sketch from the North-West, showing the future Chapel.

KEIR HETT. F.R.I.B.A.
of SEARLE & SEARLE July 19

Like so many other Peacehaven churches, the Church of England's first building in the town was constructed mainly of asbestos. It served the town well and when in the late 1950s a new church was erected the old one continued in use as the church hall. This illustration from 1954 shows the proposed new church which was built on a dominant site at the junction of Steyning Avenue, Bramber Avenue and Arundel Road.

The finished new Anglican church, easily recognizable from the prototype drawing. It is very heartening today to see that the church is well attended by younger people and it is a pleasure to attend the monthly 'family' service.

The new Roman Catholic church in Edith Avenue, also well attended. Once again, the Catholic church expanded from earlier premises which are now used as a church hall. The original mission was founded at Newhaven in 1895 with the Peacehaven Mission being established in the early 1920s.

Interior view of the church of the Ascension. Miss Horton, Mr Laycock, Mr Whitmill are among the loyal members of the congregation.

The choir and congregation process along the Arundel Road. The white houses are still in existence today, having been turned into flats. The old building in the background is the Peacehaven Electric Light Company workshop.

The choir at the church of the Ascension during a service.

The dedication ceremony for the laying of the foundation stone for the new church. The ceremony was well attended.

Another view of the stone laying ceremony, showing well the large gathering for the occasion. The large stone supported by a plank bears the inscription recording the event.

Peacehaven once had two mills, one at the western end of the Highway and this one at the eastern end of what is known today as Meeching Down, at the top of Union Hill. It was originally known as Bollen's Mill; after the death of Mr Bollen it was bought by Stones of Newhaven and was referred to as Stones Mill. It was a post mill similar to the one built at Hammondean. The old mill was dismantled and re-erected at Chailey where it now rests for all to see.

Five

Wrecks, Rescues and the Lifeboat Inn

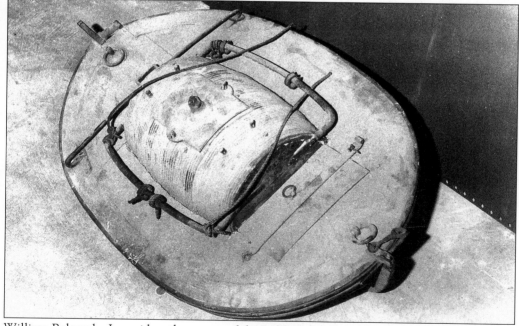

William Balcombe Langridge, the owner of the Lifeboat Inn, was very concerned with the loss of life from shipwreck and he proposed the construction of a shaft through which a lifecar could be lowered on a stout hawser. The idea proved not to be practical as there was no way of controlling the vessel. The idea was dropped and Mr Langridge instead sponsored the first lifeboat at Newhaven in 1803. The model lifecar illustrated was found in the reserve collection at the Maritime Museum. It is in fact the proposed lifecar of Mr Langridge, named the *Messenger*.

The need for some form of device for assisting shipwrecked mariners was brought to the attention of the public in 1800 when HMS *Brazen*, an eighteen-gun sloop of war engaged on channel patrol duties, ran aground just off Chene Gap with the loss of all but one of the crew. The rescued man was, by a strange quirk of fate, a non-swimmer: he tied himself to a gun slide and was washed ashore. As he reached the safety of the shore he was taken into the basket of a cliff crane which had been dragged to the cliff top. (Picture courtesy of Ted Shipsey)

The impressive *Brazen* memorial in St Michael's churchyard at the port of Newhaven. The tablets around the stone tell of the crew, the voyage and their fate, and marks the spot chosen to commemorate this great disaster. Captain John Hanson was the master of *Brazen* and although only twenty-four years of age, he was a vastly experienced seaman. His body was never found. His wife came to Newhaven seventy-four years after the memorial had been erected and lived to be 103.

The old Lifeboat Inn was rebuilt in around 1806 and with the coming of the coast blockade for the prevention of smuggling it passed into the hands of the service for use as a Preventive Station and office for the Comptroller of Customs. James Snudden (1836-1880) was for years the Chief Coastguard at Portobello and in fact his great granddaughter, Mrs Christine Smith, was born at Saltdean in the Coastguard Cottages.

A cliff crane and limber, c. 1920. The cranes were used for the first recorded time to assist shipwrecked mariners at the *Brazen* incident. Details were well recorded in the *Illustrated London News*. Later, a Mr Johnson of Brighton constructed his own cliff cranes which did great service on our coast. The last surviving one was at Saltdean where it was used as a crane to carry out works to the cliff face. Seen here is the mobile carrying unit which would usually be drawn by oxen, and in the background is a crane after being erected.

After being dragged to the cliff edge by oxen, the crane would be fixed to the ground by stout iron pins and a basket would be lowered down to the base of the cliff using of a heavy rope reeved through a block at the end of the jib. Lifting power was provided by men, not machines. These cranes provided considerable help through the years.

A close-up view of the device showing the winch end of the crane. Halfway along the main frame of the crane can be seen a locating 'pawl' to steady the rope.

The Lifeboat Inn and Comptroller of Customs' house at Portobello. The main Dover road, now the A259, is surfaced merely with rolled chalk. The long building in front of the inn is supposed to have been intended to house the lifeboat proposed by Mr Langridge. To the left are the Coastguard Cottages, erected around 1832 to house the coastguards who took over from the officers and men of the Coast Blockade. In the background are some of the earliest buildings erected at Telscombe Cliffs by the Cavendish Land Company.

The *Marquis of Lorne*, a steamer from Newhaven. In 1904, she left port carrying a cargo of stone bound for Cherbourg. It seems that after running some considerable distance to the west her engine broke down and she put back with every intention of trying to make her own home port. She eventually ran aground at Saltdean Gap and assistance was promptly provided by the Brighton No. 1 Lifeboat, *Sunlight No. 2*. The smaller lifeboat, *John Whittingham*, was not needed. The men in fact made their own way ashore from their own ship's boat.

In December 1929, the Newhaven lifeboat *Sir Fitzroy Clayton* received her first call for help during what were described as 'the worst storms ever recorded'. Winds were said to have reached 110mph and *Merwede* ran aground on the east beach, carrying bricks for the Peacehaven Company. She fetched up near to the tide mills; although the ship's resting place rendered the lifeboat useless, a line was attached swiftly by the Newhaven Life-Saving Rocket Company and the crew were all taken off with the aid of the breeches buoy. The Rocket Company received many thanks for their prompt service.

The largest vessel to be stranded in the area was the *Nimbo* (3,870 tons), which was an empty Italian cargo vessel that was driven ashore at the outfall near Portobello during the storms of November 1929. The lifeboat, *Sir Fitzroy Clayton* put to sea to render assistance but due to the high seas and the position of the *Nimbo* right on the outfall, the crew were unable to render assistance. The Newhaven Life-Saving Rocket Company were called and managed to rescue the crew of thirty using the breeches buoy. The cost of repairs to the sewer outfall was £12,500. The author's grandfather was coxswain of the Newhaven lifeboat and the Captain of the *Nimbo* gave him, as a token of thanks, a kitten that had been born on board some weeks earlier. The cat, called *Nimbo* (of course), is well remembered.

This view shows well the desperate position in which the *Nimbo* found herself on being stranded. It is little wonder that the lifeboat could not get alongside during the attempted rescue.

The men of the Coastguard who performed, at great risk to themselves, the rescue of the crews of the *Nimbo* and the *Merwede*. The shield was awarded by the Board of Trade to Newhaven lifeboat station. The officers are: Station Officer B. King, Coastguards Ramson, H. Vacher and W. Sherwood.

A local cottage industry in those early days was 'bouldering'. Small, round blue flints were picked off the beach by hand and taken to the silica works at Newhaven where they were ground up before being sent to the potteries at Stoke for final treatment to be made into domestic scouring powder. Seen here are Steve Winder and Liz Harvey collecting flints from the base of the cliffs.

The unique way to the beach at Telscombe cliffs. At the cliff end of Central Avenue there was originally a spiral staircase through the chalk cliff down to the beach. Erosion took this away in time and it was replaced by these steps.

Six
Shops, Workshops and Workers

The street enumerator registered this property as 189 South Coast Road yet for years it has always been called No. 1 Steyning Avenue. Next door the old Downs Library is just visible. The original building is still there today and it has been given a sympathetic extension eastwards. Outside the shop is Mrs Cissy Marriott, wife of well-known local 'Duke' Marriott. In later years the premises became a shop with a cafeteria adjoining; behind there was a printer's works.

'Ole man Parker' was a well-known shopkeeper, businessman and friend of Peacehaven. He started his earliest business as the first post office in town before taking over these new premises as Telscombe post office. The building is still stands today. He was a premier Peacehaven pioneer and his name is worthy of remembrance.

This was a small but busy shop on the main road, belonging to an early pioneer, Flo Fowler. It formed an important part of Sussex Place and looks much the same today. This shop has been, at various times, a radio store, a pet shop and, for a long time, a florist's.

Mr Evans was the local chemist and he lived in Friars Avenue at a house called Gwynfa. Later the business passed Reg Williamson, who grew to become a friend to all. Many early Peacehaveners would rather go and see Reg for advice than their own doctor.

For a long time there were no public houses in Peacehaven. Burden's Pioneer Stores obtained an off-licence to sell alcoholic refreshment and filled this gap in local provision. The Estate Company employed over 1,000 very thirsty workers in those golden days and Burden's did good business! This property is now Roy's liquor store.

'Kenny's Corner', a group of four shops all run by Bill Kenny, who was not only a local businessman but also a councillor, guide and mentor. The property was later altered and developed when it was granted an alcohol licence. It was known first as the County Bridge Club, later the Premier Club before becoming a pub called the Gay Highlander. It is now the Sussex Coaster.

As Peacehaven grew and businesses prospered, more and more national names came to town. These were the Westminster (later NatWest) Bank's first premises at Peacehaven. This property now houses the Tandoori Nights Indian restaurant.

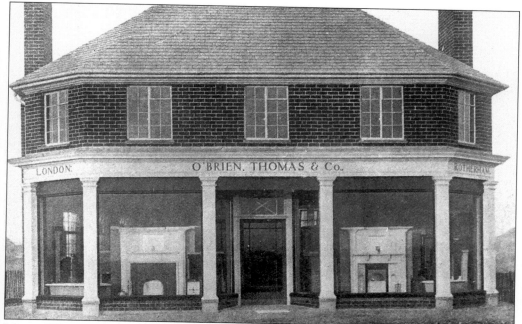

Messrs O'Brien, Thomas & Co. settled in the booming Peacehaven as builders' merchants and they built these fine premises at the eastern end of the town. Today this is the Gas Log Fire shop and the flooring shop.

Harry Mun Gavin established himself as an early estate and land agent on the site of 226 South Coast Road, the Phillip Man block. It was on a very prominent corner of the main town centre of Peacehaven near was locally called 'the Broadway'. The property changed hands over the years and went on to become the home of Reg Standing and latterly, the office of Gatward & Co., one of the town's pre-eminent solicitors.

The 1,000 and more employees of the Estate Company and its subsidiaries not only needed feeding and refreshing, but they needed transport around the various estates. Here workers return home in an Estate lorry after a good day's work. Many were lodged in temporary 'doss' houses' on the Company's premises.

The early temporary workshops of the Estate Company were soon replaced by more permanent structures, including these joiners' workshops in the company's yard. The building was large and the site stretched from the Coast Road down to the Promenade and from Sunview Avenue to Mayfield Avenue. It is possible that the staircase being constructed is for the Hotel Peacehaven and that the overseer in the black coat is 'French Henry' of Newhaven.

The many workers of the Estate Company were referred to as the Company 'Busy Bees'. This group was employed making concrete blocks. Among those present are Bill Callow and Tom Schofield, at the far left of the picture.

The Peacehaven Water Company was one of the largest of the Estate Company's subsidiaries and it was also always very busy. At one time there was such a demand for water supplies that pipes were laid directly onto the ground which meant that the supplied water was often rather warm! A stalwart of those golden days was Sandy Watts, seen in the foreground with the spade.

The Water Company always had the best of equipment, which it needed to supply the rapidly growing town. The digging of literally miles of trenches and then filling them in required a huge amount of manual labour in the days before widespread mechanization.

One of Peacehaven's most loyal supporters and earliest shopkeepers was Stan Sayer. He came to Peacehaven after the First World War, having been invalided out of the army. He set up shop in what must have seemed the middle of nowhere. Since then the town has grown. Stan's little shop later became the public house 'McKellar' and latterly, the oddly named 'Good Companions'.

Seven

Telscombe: Cliffs and Village

The Telscombe Cliffs Estate was begun before Peacehaven. It was built to a fairly good standard for the time by Cavendish Land Company. Peacehaven was still a mere thought in Neville's mind but once started, the growing and the burgeoning town soon needed water. The wells sunk in various parts of the town proved insufficient, so the moribund Telscombe Cliffs Company was acquired by the Peacehaven Company for its water. There was a well beneath what is now the kitchen floor of the school in Telscombe Cliffs Way. This is the Telscombe Cliffs post office (later to become the Cliffs Club) with a donkey cart for deliveries. The property has now been demolished and a new office block is being erected for Telscombe Town Council.

On the South Coast Road, westward of the earlier post office, stood Mr Cartwright's estate office. He was a house, land and estate agent as well as a builders' merchant and developer. Mr Cartwright is seated further from the camera in the cart. The adjoining post office went on to be the Estate Company's western office. It was later a hotel (known to the locals as the White Hotel) for a time and then a training base for firemen, before becoming the Cliffs Club, a popular social venue.

Telscombe Tye Estate

FREEHOLD BUNGALOWS

TYPE A £650
With Garage £690

TYPE C £640

200 YDS.
SEA AND DOWNS

TYPE B £650

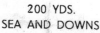

12 MINS. BUS SERVICE
to BRIGHTON STATION

£65 DEPOSIT & 17/3
PER WEEK

EDGERTON : BUILDER
Telscombe Cliffs, Sussex

TYPE D £650

Jack Edgerton was a well-known builder. He had workshops and offices in Buckhurst Road in what later became the Unique Slide Rule Company and then Cliff Plastics. He built good quality homes all over the estate and this postcard shows the variety available.... If only the prices were the same today!

The White Hotel and café. The estate now shows an advanced state of development since being taken over by the Peacehaven Company, with metalled roads and street lighting. Next to the hotel is Mr Cartwright's home and offices. The flag sign is a bus stop for the Southdown Bus Company. The smart Southdown buses in their livery of green with gold signwriting were a feature of the coast road in those times.

Looking west past the hotel, with the South Coast Road winding up over the Tye. This is still in the period before the road was properly surfaced. In the background is the Portobello Outfall house, just beyond the old Comptroller of Customs' house and Lifeboat Inn (which is now the Badger's Watch).

Ambrose Gorham, the sporting squire of Telscombe, was a rather shy and retiring man and he is rarely seen in group photographs. Here he stands with the village children about to lay a foundation stone or begin a repair, possibly to the village club.

The school in Telscombe was not very big, even at its biggest and best. The keen young pupils here are, from left to right, back row: Ginny Swann, Beryl Woodford, Lily Tiller, Peggy Digby, Jim Okines, Frank Bullock, Clara Moore. Front row: Clive Sutton, Clifford Moore, Pearl Okines, Bertie Moor, Pearl Nelson, Joan Lambert.

This rudimentary seaplane taking off at Newhaven Harbour is the plane owned and flown by the early aviator Claude Graham White who was based at Hendon. He was in Newhaven to see at first hand the record-breaking cross-channel run by RMS *Paris IV* in 1913. The passenger who flew with Graham White was none other than Ambrose Gorham. It is interesting to note that today's fast Lynx vessels can cross the channel in around 2hr 20mins, only 12mins faster than the *Paris IV* in 1913.

Telscombe is a quintessential English village, tucked away in a fold of the downs. sitting as it were on Peacehaven's shoulder, it has seen little change since the days of Ambrose Gorham. He loved the old village for its simplicity, its quietude, its very Englishness.

Bankside Cottages and the ivy-covered church in Telscombe, possibly in the 1920s. The flags suggest that this was Empire Day. In the road is a prize Sussex bullock from Gorman's estate, being led by its farmer.

Telscombe village on Hunt Day, a tradition widely supported before the Second World War, particularly in rural areas. The road is lined with the cars and carriages of the participating gentry and the hunt is setting off with the hounds in front.

The hunt in front of the old church of St Lawrence. The ivy that so fully clothes the walls is well trimmed. In the church are two crosses carved onto two pillars in memory of two knights who left Telscombe to fight in the Crusades in the twelfth century.

The church and Bankside Cottages seem strangely quiet and deserted, even for such a rural setting. This tranquil winter or autumn scene makes it difficult to imagine the Roman camp which was once situated here.

Ambrose Gorham, squire of Telscombe, always did his best to look after the inhabitants whom he looked upon as friends. For them all he had built this wonderful club house for the use and the enjoyment of the villagers. In the old days, inside the club, cups and trophies from the squire's sporting exploits were displayed. Long may he be remembered.

A final 1920s view of Telscombe, on the road which leads from the Lewes Road and winds its way south through the village. The gateway on the right is the vicarage.

Eight
Greater Peacehaven

The Cliffs near Brighton.

It was Charles Neville, the founder of Peacehaven, who coined the phrase 'Greater Peacehaven' to include the developments at Saltdean, Newhaven, Rottingdean and similar places. This early view of Saltdean looking eastwards towards the Tye shows that the development had not yet reached this far along the coast. There are a few houses in Hamsey Road in the distance. Note the amazing (at least by today's standards) amount of greensward on the south of the coast road.

Saltdean is now growing; however, the main road (now the A259) is very narrow indeed and it is mostly fenced off. On the south of the road is the Smugglers' Haunt cafeteria where the pillars have only just been erected; it is thought that they were bought from an exhibition in London. The former estate office can be seen as can the old Coastguard Cottages.

These tennis courts were built on the site of today's swimming pool and lido. On the right is the early estate office, later to be offered as a Gift House. The ubiquitous Estate flag flies in the centre of the picture. Saltdean was, without doubt, one of the best of Neville's developments.

Sussex oxen being used to gather in the hay before the advent of mechanized farming practices.

Oxen or bullocks were harnessed in pairs and they were trained to the yoke from early days. They were part of a tradition of subsistence agriculture dating back to Saxon times and before.

The Ocean Hotel at Saltdean, one of Neville's finest creations. As can be seen it was very large; in later years it was acquired by Butlin's as a holiday resort hotel and it has only recently been radically changed. In place of the tennis courts there is now the lido which could be said to rival even its continental counterparts. Designed and built in the 'curvilinear' style, the lido was at once an attraction to many. The pool itself could cope with 200 bathers and the blue-tiled floor and sides made it at once attractive. The decks, boards and attendant amenities could be compared to those on the deck of a fashionable liner. It was a great asset to 'Greater Peacehaven'.

The Valley at North Peacehaven has always been a haven of peace and tranquillity. Set aside for agricultural smallholdings, it has taken longer than most of the rest of the area to attract the ever-impatient hand of the developer. It is the one place where the old atmosphere of Neville's Peacehaven can still be found.

One of the biggest problems facing the emergent Peacehaven was the lack of made roads and main drains. This caused a great deal of bad feeling and rancour which lasted for many years. Charles Neville was determined that this should not be the case in his new developments at Saltdean. There was an abundance of road-making material available on site in the form of flints. This is an early team of roadmakers at work with steam road rollers, delivery carts etc.

Neville opened the Hotel Peacehaven on a grand scale and fully in keeping with his ideas of making the most of the occasion. There were concerts, dances, firework displays, bonfires, much eating and drinking and entertaining and every opportunity was taken to extol the virtues of the hotel, and of course, the new Garden City of amazing growth. Neville also booked the services of Anton Fokker, who demonstrated his skill with the glider pictured here as part of the celebrations.

When the Rottingdean Heights estate was developed there was considerable interest shown and in fact the Company had to erect temporary offices in a tent. This is the more formal and more permanent office which succeeded the tent, together with the ever-present Peacehaven flag.

A page from an early edition of the *Peacehaven Post*, the Estate Company's house magazine, showing as it does many of the town's leading traders. Sadly, perhaps, the only business listed here which is still trading today at Peacehaven is Mr Wagstaff. Mr Barnard the builder has an interesting advertisement telling us that bungalows were available from £375!

Nine
Sports and Peacehaven People

At the cessation of hostilities in 1945 it did not take long for this enthusiastic group of local people to get together for a party. Many of them were keen sportsmen, many were town shopkeepers or just grateful townsfolk. This party was held in Lureland Hall, opposite the Hotel Peacehaven. Seated on the right is Revd Martyn Harris, Vicar of Telscombe. Opposite him is Mr Wilmhurst and behind Revd Harris are two other well-known Peacehaveners – Sid Mepstead the butcher and Mr Woodruff, a well-known 'wordsmith'.

The opening ceremony for Peacehaven's new sports ground in 1979. The ribbon was cut by the well-known Sussex cricketer Peter Graves, with the mayor and other dignitaries applauding. The sports park was the result of a lot of effort from a lot of people; Peacehaven's MP, Tim Rathbone, was particularly influential.

Here the author, in his capacity as town mayor, bids welcome to the large concourse of people who made the most of the sunny weather on the day of the opening ceremony for the sports ground.

Football has always played an important part in the life of Peacehaven, even from early days. This is the Peacehaven first team in around 1930. Many of the players were also members of the cricket team at the change of seasons. Many of these man worked for the Company in Peacehaven. Included here are Dick Gosling, Michael Groves, Duncan Stoten and Arthur Blake. The goalkeeper, Jack Burgess, continued playing for many years.

Peacehaven First again, some years later. Jack Burgess is still the goalkeeper; Dick Gosling is in the centre with his hand on the ball. Second from the right on the back row is Ron Bassett, who went on to captain the team. Also present are Trevor Redshaw and Vern Parris.

The cricket eleven was made up of many of the football eleven; this picture includes Mr Stoten, Dick Gosling, Arthur Blake, Michael Wood, Willy Parks, Mr Wilds, Bubbles Sutton, Mr Troak and Mr Durrant.

An annual dinner of the Peacehaven Football Club in the dining room of the Hotel Peacehaven.

The Peacehaven troop of Boy Scouts was formed in the mid-1920s; they are seen here wearing the hats which were the norm in the early days of the Scouting movement. The troop grew as the town grew and they are still very active in Peacehaven today.

Peacehaven Scouts shortly after the Second World War, at the old Scout hut on what is today's 'Joff' site. The Scoutmaster was Mr Simpson and he is flanked by Arthur Drapper and Alfie Smith. Behind him is a young Martin Delacourt. Those in the front row include George Wagstaff and John Giles.

Even in the earliest days, one of the town's amenities was the beach and later the tidal pool. The beach is seen here in the 1920s or 1930s. Note the number of people wearing hats even in an informal, recreational setting such as this.

The Peacehaven Philharmonic and Operatic Society was very successful and they promoted fine productions under the very able tutelage of their leader and conductor, Felix Powell (seen here with baton in hand). They specialized in Gilbert and Sullivan; this is a performance of *HMS Pinafore* in 1930.

Felix Powell (front row in the orchestra pit, facing right) was perhaps best remembered for writing the popular First World War song, 'Pack up your troubles in your old kit bag'. He wrote a number of local songs for the Estate Company such as 'Lureland Waltz' and 'Come to Peacehaven!'. These did not receive wide acclaim. This production is probably *Yeomen of the Guard* during the 1930s.

The wedding of Joan Gosling, a nurse at the Gracie Fields Children's Home and Orphanage, and Eddie Turner, a prominent Peacehaven builder, on 26 April 1952. Joan Turner still lives in Peacehaven.

A stalwart of the church of the Ascension was the Revd Long (left), who served the parish long and faithfully. He played a very active part in all Peacehaven activities.

Mr Frank Pegler (nearer the camera) came to Peacehaven to work for the South Coast Land & Resort Company in Peacehaven's formative years. He was highly regarded by Charles Neville and he was responsible for much of the laying out of Peacehaven. On leaving the Estate Company he went to work for the Brighton Corporation and is seen here in their drawing office.

For many years Peacehaven held an annual fair, including a procession of floats and marchers. This decorated commercial vehicle (by Wagstaff's) is making reference to the fact that the Rural District Council had just given permission for public conveniences to be erected in the town centre, on a prominent site. *Clochmerle* was then showing in Brighton and provided a convenient link. The driver is Jack Wagstaff and on board are (from left to right) Miss Noreen Wagstaff, Tony Payne, Percy Cornford and Paul Cornford.

Steyning Avenue from the main South Coast Road. The vacant site on the corner is now occupied by Lureland Court. The adults are Dorothy Penn and her brother David.

The VE Day party was well attended by many Peacehaven children – the grown-ups had their own party! This was in Lureland Hall. Among those present are Jimmy Buck, Shirley Parsons and Miss Parker – no doubt readers will recognize many more.

The gentleman on the right, looking westwards along the beach, is Mr Paul White of Chailey Rural District Council, who for many years administered Peacehaven.

For many years Peacehaven had to make its own entertainment, always with its own talented performers. This is Mrs Nessie Sankey in 1951; she was a very prominent supportive player for local organizations.

This performance of *Cinderella* after the war was very successful. The actors are, from left to right: Mrs De Monti, Mrs Goodwin, Mrs Kathleen Taylor, Mrs Stevens and Mrs Oates.

An evening gathering in the garden of Fourways, which was a popular meeting place for many years and home of the local Senior Citizens' Group. The properties in the background are easily identifiable: there is the Barrett Brothers shop and old tin stable, St Mary Le Bridge is right behind and on The Promenade are The Gables and a white bungalow called Tinker Bell, the erstwhile home of Charles Neville.

The production of *Aladdin* in 1951 was well supported and well received and it had a considerable cast. From left to right, far right back row: Amy Goodwin, Peggy Burke, Janice Noakes. Back row: Mrs De Monti, Marion Mercer, Kathleen Taylor, Renee Winter, Eve Oates, Jo Jones, Rosemary Tucknott, Dorothy Turner, Daisy Stevens, -?-, -?-, Betty Goodwin, Nessie Sankey. Centre: Gillian Bryant, Judith Harrison, Beryl Chalmers. Front row: Pat Winter, Rona Burdett, Trudie Coppinger, Jill Wagstaff, Rose Hickford, Christine De Monti, Barbara King.

Form 3A, Newhaven Girls' School, in July 1948. From left to right, back row: Eileen Row, Jennifer Harrison, Phyllis Digby, Pat Hood, Iris Harvey, Margaret Sanders, Yvonne Etherington, Josie Hooper, Irene Adams, Doreen Medhurst. Middle row: Sheila Sherlock, Jennifer Cole, Jeanette Croucher, Christine Bartholomew, Sheila Gisborne, -?-, Gwen Anderson. Front row: Lilian Mitchell, Sheila Deacon, Vivienne Lower, Beryl Eager, Sylvia Brown, Edith Butler, Audrey Lower, Janice Sutton Gow.

The Hotel Peacehaven used its Italianate gardens whenever possible for a variety of occasions. This appears to be May Day with a maypole on the left and schoolchildren enjoying themselves.

The 'old tin school' was very much a part of everyday Peacehaven life. It was situated at the end of Roundhay Road between Cissbury and Downland Avenues, the site of today's Hoathdown House. The staff in the early 1930s are from left to right: Miss Tynan, Miss Wheatley, Mr Blackman (headmaster), Mr Joe Funnell, Miss Barratt.

The school was proud of its pupils' competitive achievements and on the steps are the netball team, runners-up in the East Sussex League in 1930. The board is held by Miss Valerie Wagstaff and Mr Blackman stands behind. The old school served Peacehaven well and it was a sad loss when it closed.

Jack Lewis was the largest man in the South's Home Guard units and he was a member of the Peacehaven and Telscombe 'Dad's Army'. He is seen here with John Wood, member of a well known pioneer Peacehaven family. It was his father, Luther Wood, who started the first family business in the early days of the town.

Young David Fowler went on to be the manager of the Pavilion Theatre when it was a cinema. This valuable local amenity was lost to the town when it burned down in 1939. David's father was a local builder known to all as Alf. His mother had a florist's on the main road and she owned the first new bungalow that was built in Peacehaven after the war. His sister, Dorothy, a stalwart of the Historical Society, ran a cafeteria for some years at Peacehaven.

The Hotel Peacehaven as refurbished in the 1960s. Under the benign guidance of its proprietor, Mr Roger Lythgoe, the hotel played a very important part in everyday life for the town, hosting many parties and gatherings.

The badge of the original Peacehaven & Telscombe Cricket Club. Residents are now hopeful that the Cricket Club may be revived – it certainly deserves a place in Peacehaven. John Copper, a local licensee and business man, tried valiantly to support and promote a club in the 1990s.

Ten

'Homes Fit for Heroes'

The work of the Company artist, Gordon Volk, was to be found not only in the many publications of the South Coast Land & Resort Company but also in many advertisements that appeared in guide books, publicity journals and advertising campaigns. This is one of Volk's typical offerings; drawn in 1922, it shows his version of a typical Peacehaven bungalow with large laid out garden, clear skies etc.

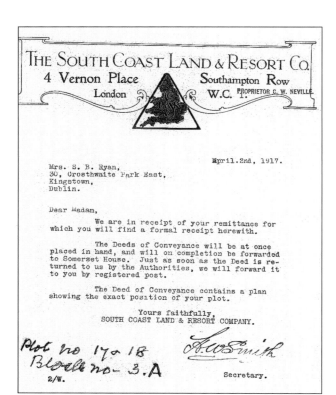

Mrs Ryan was one of the many winners in the great competition to put forward a name for the 'New Garden City by the Sea' in 1917. Instead of the fifty free plots originally intended and advertised by the company, there were 2,500. However, each lucky winner was charged for the Deed of Conveyance on their property!

This receipt, issued in April 1917, acknowledges Mrs Ryan's payment of £4 4s (four guineas) for the deed. Contestants were told in the original competition details that the charge would be three guineas!

RECEIPT.   No. P **141**

The South Coast Land and Resort Company.

PROPRIETOR: C. W. NEVILLE.

Received of *Mrs Sarah Blackwood Ryan.*

of *30 Crosthwaite Park East Kingstown. Dublin*

the Sum of *Four Guineas.* being payment in full for

a Building Plot at Peacehaven, which is to include a Deed of

Conveyance with the Government Stamp Duty paid.

For and behalf of

THE SOUTH COAST LAND AND RESORT COMPANY.

£ 4 : 4 :

Date *2nd April 1917.*   Secretary.

NOTE.—The usual time for the preparation and completion of a Deed of Conveyance is about thirty days. The Deed will be forwarded to you by registered post immediately it is returned to us from Somerset House duly stamped.

South Coast Land & Resort Co., Ltd.,

PEACEHAVEN, SUSSEX.

Walter Gillett, Ltd., Printers, Brighton.

No. *15842*   *Sept 5* 192*4*

Received *of Mrs S B Ryan*

the sum of *Two pounds ten shillings*

being the Amount paid in respect to the ~~Purchase~~ *Reserving* of Plots *17/18*

in Block *3A* .... Estate

For and on behalf of SOUTH COAST LAND & RESORT CO., LTD.

£ *2 = 10 = 0*

WITH THANKS.   Cashier.

This further receipt issued in 1924 advises that Mrs Ryan has now been charged a further £2 10s for 'reserving' her land. Originally she would have won just a single plot so it seems that she purchased the adjoining plot to make an adequate building site. Most of the 'Prize Plot' lands were never built on, as there were no made roads, no drainage and no utilities.

The first bungalows built in the new Peacehaven at the end of the First World War, the first 'Homes for Heroes'. They were of rather substandard construction and for many years there were no roads, no drainage, no street lighting etc. People were moved to say that you had to be a hero to live in one of these homes but Neville, in his own defence, said 'at least I gave them somewhere to live'. These were in Seaview Avenue between the South Coast Road and the Arundel Road.

This is very typical of Peacehaven in the 1920s and '30s. The roads are still unmade, drainage is still by cesspool and there are no street lights but still people poured down to settle in Peacehaven. The house on the right was built as a small hotel and called Jevington House. It is in Phyllis Avenue at the junction with Arundel Road. It is now two flats.

Neville had built for himself a very fine bungalow on the Promenade, on a high spot at the junction of Bolney Avenue and the Promenade. This he called Tinker Bell. The views were nothing short of amazing, the interior was finished just as one would expect and it was built at the same time as the Hotel Peacehaven and in a similar style.

This property served not only as a family home but also as a butcher's shop, the business of Mr Luther Wood, a well known early Arcadian. The business moved to bigger, better and more central premises but the bungalow is still a fine home, at the corner of Southdown Avenue and the Coast Road.

The house built by the Peacehaven chemist, Mr Evans, in Friars Avenue. He called it Gwynfa and it still stands today, with a few alterations.

The more primitive side of Peacehaven was inland, in what the locals called 'Indian country'. In Gold Lane, named after the Company architect, Chas Gold, a bungalow was built in the late 1920s called The Turrets. It was constructed to an unusual design, with the outer walls in corrugated iron. At each end there were turrets, or belvederes, also of corrugated iron. The passage of time has not been kind in this case and this is all is left today of The Turrets.

HAPPY HOMES IN
RODERICK AVENUE,
PEACEHAVEN.

At the southern end of Roderick Avenue a number of very good quality homes were built and many still stand today. The building is little changed today, although there is a made road now and the exterior paintwork is different.

The Peacehaven Building & Supply Company was a limb of the South Coast Land & Resort Company. They always strove to improve on their products and this bungalow, one of three in Cavell Avenue, was intended to show the way ahead for construction. The main interior walls were cast in concrete away from the site and placed on the pre-laid concrete foundations. In the early days concrete was seen as an ideal new building material for this kind of house, but disadvantages were later discovered.

This is a pre-war house that was built in Arundel Road as one of a pair. It has stood the test of time and together with its twin it has been converted into flats. It was for many years the local sweep's house, in the days when coal fires were still commonplace.

The Peacehaven Estate ended at Cornwall Avenue, by the 'Pylons', and the Friars Bay Building Estate started at Seaview Road. It was originally described as being at 'Newhaven-on-Sea'! This house, on the corner of Bayview Road, is a typical example of the good quality bungalows that were built at the time.

The Okines were early settlers at Peacehaven and they had this rather fine bungalow right at the back in Phyllis Avenue, north of Telscombe Road. It stood next to what was known for years as 'the railway reservation', a reminder of the early aspirations to extend the railway system to the Garden City.

A plan of one style of early
Peacehaven bungalows offered
for sale by the Company. It is,
to say the least, 'scant'. Today
the whole bungalow would fit
into a good-sized lounge.
There is no bathroom and no
inside toilet but it was said to
be 'sound and snug'. (Picture:
Tony Payne)

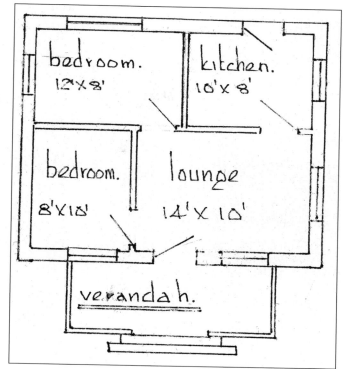

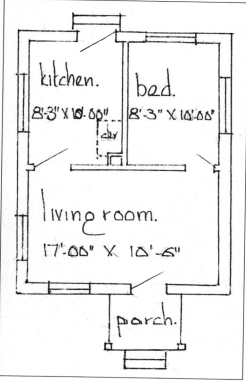

It is a moot point whether this is a better
example than the plan above. A little larger,
perhaps, but still no bathroom or toilet
facilities. Were these really 'homes fit for
heroes'? (Picture: Tony Payne)

This was said to be the first brick-built bungalow in Peacehaven, constructed in around 1923. Previous designs had used asbestos and corrugated iron. It seems to be substantial and spacious and is on high ground.

It did not take long for people to ask for something better than they were being shown. Also freelance building companies started to arrive (much to Mr Neville's annoyance) and they put up better properties as the availability of building materials improved. This is Tresco, erected in a first-class spot south of the main coast road.

This aerial photograph shows well the now expanding and burgeoning estate. Most avenues have a number of properties and the main road is starting to fill up. Apart from the main road, the roads are still unmade.

Frimley Green, the family bungalow of Mr Reg Standing in Horsham Avenue. He was one of the early pioneer builders in Peacehaven. The house was soundly built and not unattractive, but it was demolished to make way for new homes.

Estate Regulations.

There are residents—well-intentioned people, who have perhaps felt aggrieved at times because it has been necessary for us to insist upon the stipulations and conditions under which land at Peacehaven is purchased, being carried out. To such we can only say that playing the part of policemen to the Estate is far from congenial to us. How necessary it is you can judge from the unsightly coloured advertising sign-boards which have recently appeared on the Estate, which would, if not removed, prove a detriment to Peacehaven by creating a bad impression upon visitors, who will naturally imagine that the ugly hoardings seen in the outskirts of many large cities will become a feature of our Garden City.

Again, there are the individuals who have erected builders' sheds and are endeavouring to carry on a builder's business on residential plots contrary to their agreements, and one or two others who are endeavouring to carry on business on land sold for residential purposes only. In some cases it has been necessary for us to begin legal proceedings, which will be followed in all other cases unless the offending premises are removed. In doing this we are acting in the interests of all the residents, and we would point out that unless such regulations were enforced that Peacehaven, instead of becoming a model settlement, would become a town of shacks and hoardings which would rapidly destroy all possibility of making it the ideal Garden City at which we have consistently aimed.

We look for the support of all people of goodwill to assist us in carrying out these very necessary regulations.

SOUTH COAST LAND & RESORT CO., LTD.

The Estate Regulations. Mr Neville was regularly writing to residents telling them what they could and could not do. He particularly reminded people about unofficial sheds, builders' yards etc. and he was particularly antagonistic towards other builders, feeling that they were depriving him of business that should have been his. There is a well-known case in which he cut off the water supply to a family home because the owner dared to run a builders' yard and estate agency. The water remained disconnected for nearly a year before the legal process found in favour of the defendant.

Eleven
Some Peacehaven Worthies

Charles William Neville in later years. By this time his 'Greater Peacehaven' had grown to become a large, though sprawling, town. Saltdean had grown to become what was often referred to as 'Brighton's fairest sister'. In his later years Neville seldom visited Peacehaven; he even said that at times he 'feared for his life' – but that was customary Charles Neville exaggeration.

The Wagstaff family grew up in early Peacehaven. Isaac worked as a carpenter at the marine workshops at Newhaven harbour as well as running a business in Peacehaven as an estate agent, builder and funeral director. He and his wife, Eva, raised their family in God-fearing ways through a lot of adversity and hardship and they will be remembered as one of the town's best-known families. At the back are Harold Wagstaff and his father, Isaac; in the centre are daughters Louie and Kathy and with Mrs Wagstaff at the front are the two youngest children, Valerie and Jack.

The man seated on this attractive float in the town carnival is Gordon Volk, the Company artist.

Reg Standing came to Peacehaven to work for the Estate Company and he then set up in business on his own account as a builder and contractor. He was, himself a very talented carpenter and joiner and did much of the interior woodwork at the Hotel Peacehaven. Reg Standing was a prominent member of the early Peacehaven Lodge of Freemasons.

John Standing carried on where his father left off and is still running a building and decorating business in Peacehaven. He is seen here at the family home with his 'Ner-a-car', a strange device more like a motorbike than a car; this automotive oddity was much used by district nurses.

Young John Wood, son of Luther, one of the early settlers in Peacehaven. He later followed in his father's footsteps and became a well-known and respected butcher.

'Duke' Marriott, the local milkman for many years, and his wife. He served the growing township well.

The choir of the church of the Ascension, Bramber Avenue, with the church itself behind. The man in front in the ceremonial vestments is the Revd Cornelius, an early settler at Peacehaven. On his right is the respected Percy Lonsdale; next to him are Mr Woodruff and Mr Whitmill. To the minister's left is Mr Groble, and then Mr Stubbs and Mr Baker. In the back row, fourth from left, is young Ron Lonsdale who is now a well-known accountant in the town.

The official opening of the Newhaven & Seaford Historical Society Museum on the seafront at Newhaven. On the right is a well known and respected Peacehaven Pioneer, Bob Poplett. He is known for his active work over many years recording Peacehaven's unique history. On the left is the author.

The name of 'Copper' is synonymous with Peacehaven in the same way that it is synonymous with folk music. The family lived at Rottingdean for many years before Bob settled in Peacehaven. He is an accomplished writer, painter, musician and singer. His family all followed in his footsteps. Here is Bob seated with his son John on the left, daughter Jill centre and son-in-law, Jon, on the right. Bob's grandchildren now also sing with great enthusiasm.

Jim and Margaret Palmer are a well-known and popular Peacehaven couple. Jim was a builder and contractor for many years as well as being a popular licensee. Jim's mother was a school headmistress.

Stan Sayers and his wife came to Peacehaven in the very early days. Stan was invalided out of the Army after being wounded in the First World War and the young couple set up in business at Downland Stores, just by the 'Bricky', the early brickmaking works. Stan said that when he moved in he could see just three roofs from his front door.

Commander Davenport RN lived in the emergent town almost from the beginning. It was he who realized that Peacehaven sat astride the Greenwich Meridian and he campaigned successfully to have a monument erected to mark the spot on the Promenade. Seen here are, from left to right: Mrs Davenport, Dorothy Penn, Mr Davenport Jnr, Commander Davenport, -?-.

Alf Fowler was one of the early pioneers who came to Peacehaven to build homes. He was a popular figure, always seen riding his bicycle round the town in morning trousers, black blazer and black Homburg hat. His son, David, was the popular manager of the Pavilion Cinema for a number of years. His daughter, Dorothy, is a tower of strength in the local historical society.

Colin Bennet was in fact a Newhavener but settled in Peacehaven with his wife, Wendy, and family. He had businesses in Newhaven and Woodingdean and was a senior member of the local Rotary Club. He was an accomplished golfer, a keen sportsman and a very good friend. He is sadly missed.

Jack and Margaret Wagstaff. The Wagstaff family business dates back to the 1920s and today is certainly much respected. Margaret's father was a schoolteacher and headmaster.

Eva and Tom Claxton came to Peacehaven from Brighton. They would never claim to be 'Pioneers' in the real sense but they are popular members of the community.

Bob Hockey (right) was a navigator in Manchester and Lancaster bombers during the Second World War. After the war he set up in Peacehaven as a restaurateur and then established a successful building business. Bob was a very keen sportsman and it was due to his drive and enthusiasm that the Peacehaven Football Club was so successful. He was also a very enthusiastic driver of fast cars. On the left is the author.

Twelve
What of the Future?

At the cessation of hostilities in 1945 some sense of normality returned to Peacehaven. Charles Neville was still in control, but he seldom came to Peacehaven. There was an acute shortage of building materials, just as there had been at the end of the First World War. Even into the 1950s a licence had to be obtained for new work. This bungalow was the first to be rebuilt in Peacehaven at the end of the war; its predecessor, Rosalyn, had been bombed by the Italian air force. Being new and fairly modern, it set the design for a number of others. (Picture courtesy of J. Wagstaff)

When rebuilding began after the war, tried and tested plans were used. This bungalow in Bolney Avenue is basically the same as the one on p. 115. Certain facilities have been modernized, but it remains essentially the same. The need to cater for the now ubiquitous motor car has not yet arisen: there is no garage and not even a driveway. (Photograph courtesy of J. Wagstaff)

Later, developers were permitted to vary their designs more than previously. These semi-detached properties were built in Bayview Road by Mr Jack Delacourt. The passage of time has been kind and these still provide a good spacious home. (Photograph courtesy of Payne & Needham)

Another pair of semi-detached bungalows, but in a different style. While at the beginning of the 1950s car ownership was a privilege of the few, by the time these dwellings were built, car ownership was universal enough to warrant the inclusion of garages in the design. (Photograph courtesy of Payne & Needham)

As land became scarcer, houses were designed with narrower plots of land in mind – these 1960s semis in Southview Road are a good example. (Photograph courtesy Payne & Needham)

The use of designs for detached homes gave even greater scope for 'grace and space'. In this house in Sunview Avenue maximum use is now being made of the outlook. The sleeping accommodation is usefully kept apart from the living accommodation not just by walls but by space, for added soundproofing. (Photograph courtesy of Payne & Needham)

The plans used for the house in the picture above were very practical but wasteful of space. In this instance the developers used the same ground floor plan but took out wasted space and put the door in the centre, necessitating a smaller hallway. This is in Southview Road. (Photograph courtesy of Payne & Needham)

This family home in Firle Road is developed on an even narrower plot. This 'chalet-style' house has three bedrooms, a lounge, a dining room and a large kitchen as well as two toilets, a bathroom and a shower. (Photograph courtesy of A.G. Kennedy Ltd)

A further style of property, this time in Dorothy Avenue. The interior has been adjusted so that the main bedroom is on the first floor. It even has a bedroom at either end of the bathroom – a useful novelty. (Photograph courtesy of Brian Barratt and Tony Payne)

A logical development from the house on the previous page was to have an integral garage but still a lot of family room. This is in Balcombe road. (Photograph courtesy of Payne & Needham)

Houses on the Promenade, with unrivalled sea and cliff-top views, one of the most desirable places left in Peacehaven. The houses all have wide windows and conservatories, while the garage is out of sight round the corner. (Photograph courtesy of Tony Payne)

A small retirement home has been usefully fitted into a vacant area in a larger development. (Photograph courtesy of Payne & Needham)

There is an amazing contrast between the Dover Road of the 1930s, seen earlier in the book, and today's A259, seen here at Saltdean. Gone are all the open spaces, replaced by as many houses and bungalows as the developers could squeeze in.

The South Coast Road today. This is in the middle of Peacehaven with Giles' the plumbers on the right. Every available plot of land has been taken up by developments.

One of the town's nicest avenues was, in the early days, Cissbury Avenue; now it has lost it identity somewhat among the modern developments. One advantage that residents of thi avenue have, however, is that at the end is open land for miles.

On this site used to stand one of the earliest buildings in the new town, housing the offices of the South Coast Land and Resort Company. In later years it was the site of one of Peacehaven's most popular meeting and relaxing places – the Bells Club. Run by the well-known Peacehavener Jim Palmer and his family, it was almost a second home to many.

In the early days, the Promenade, the beach and the steps were all that made up Peacehaven. Since then the coast has changed a lot too. This view shows the new coastal defence works and the under-cliff walk (also used as an access route for repair and service vehicles). It is a useful amenity for many, particularly those with dogs.

One of the last bastions of the older days when space was all around in Peacehaven. This is the valley at Peacehaven. At the time of writing the future of this open space hangs in the balance, with the possibility of further developments here in the near future.

Peacehaven is not renowned for its famous residents but there have nonetheless been one or two. The young Flora Robson gave a very early public performance at the Rosemary way back in 1922. The Rosemary has now gone and a new terrace has been built in its place but a thoughtful resident, Mr Douglas Collinson, agreed that a plaque could be placed upon his wall to mark Dame Flora's place in our history.